ABCs

for

Financial Independence

Lisa Paniccia

Dedication

This book is dedicated to those who I share my dance parties with . . . you make my life rich!

Table of Contents

Introduction

If you are looking for the road to financial stability, start here. Take charge of your financial well-being. Create your financial reality.

Being financially independent does not have to be hard or complicated. Provided are some practical, commonsense principles. Knowing where to start and what to do next can help you improve your situation.

If you do nothing, then nothing will change. So, I have created some action plans that I call *Money Movement Plans*. This will allow you to practice focusing on your financial well-being. You will gain a better understanding of the principles. The Money Movement Plans contain reflection exercises, suggestions on how to get started, and attainable goals designed to create the foundation you need to move forward.

Whether you are 16, in your 60s, or anywhere in between, practice your ABCs. Feel a sense of accomplishment by becoming financially independent!

A

Accumulate

Accumulate is another word for "Add".

Taking ownership of your financial well-being has a lot to do with math. The numbers are black and white. They must make sense. They must add up. And, if you are savvy, you can harness the power of these numbers to reach your goals. There are common components to everyone's financial puzzle, however, your financial situation has its own unique set of pieces. The good news is you can figure out how to utilize those pieces to take control of your finances, and it will be immensely rewarding.

Being financially independent does not have to be complicated. For example, accumulating is good in terms of adding. Adding, in this case, means saving.

There is a certain feeling of freedom and comfort when we know we have security. Having savings can, for example, provide the freedom to choose a desired home in an ideal location, the freedom to travel, and to make important life choices, like if and where to further your education. Knowing that saving can bring peace of mind may help you to find joy in preparing for the future. You can develop a mindset where you find it gratifying to save money because that dollar bill is not just a piece of paper . . . it's a means to create the life you envision.

There are additional benefits to saving. Having money put aside will also be your safety net when financial difficulties arise. No one knows when hard times will come. It could be a health issue, a job loss, or a car repair, among other possibilities. Christopher Paolini (2011) once cautioned: "It's impossible to go through life unscathed. Nor should you want to. By the hurts we accumulate, we measure both our follies and our accomplishments." You can lay the groundwork to withstand financial struggles.

Overall, "69% of adult Americans have less than $1,000 in a **savings** account" (Huddleston, 2019). If you are a member of this group, one injury, one accident, one repair can put you in debt. This is fixable! Saving for unexpected emergencies, retirement, vacations, school (or just having extra money) can set you up to better deal with many of life's burdens. Wouldn't it be better if you didn't have to scramble to come up with the necessary money for life's predicaments? Saving is a much better strategy than being burdened with debt. There's a proverb that says: "an ounce of prevention is worth a pound of cure." Basically, this means it's better to stop something from happening in the first place than deal with the fallout. You are more likely to weather the financial setbacks that come your way *if* you have reserves set aside.

On the flip side, *accumulating* debt is not a healthy financial habit. In math terms, it is a negative. Yet, there are going to be times when debt is unavoidable. Even purchasing a used car will often require a loan. That's ok! The important part is that you formulate a plan to pay it off. You may want to include a contingency plan IF you lose your job or suffer another financial loss while you are still paying on that debt. For instance, you may need to take (subtract) money you had earmarked for a vacation. Your debt is your responsibility. If you want to be financially independent, you need to address all your finances, including the parts that are not fun.

<u>Goal</u>

√ Accumulate wealth

Don't accumulate debt

Money Movement Plan

- *Put aside some savings each month.* It doesn't have to be a large amount. If you are just starting out, aim for putting away at least 8% of your take-home pay. If you are already putting aside some savings, try putting aside a little more. Work your way up to 20%.

- *If you have debt, pay a little extra on the* **principal** *of your debt.* Contact whoever owns your debt and specify that any extra payments are to go towards the principal amount of the loan only. First, make sure there aren't any penalties associated with paying off your debt early. Since you are paying extra on your principal, as opposed to interest, you will be saving money in interest if you continue with the same extra payment on a regular basis.

- *Find a way to visualize and internalize your progress.* Maybe put a note on your refrigerator marking your progress or tell Alexa or Google to congratulate you on the first day of each month for your efforts. It's important to acknowledge the wins!

- *Set a time frame.* Choose a starting date. Hold yourself accountable for this goal. Check your progress after three to four months. During these progress checks, ask yourself:

- Was it an easy change?
- Do you feel better about having more money / less debt?
- Are you thinking about saving more / further paying down your debt?
- Do you need to make any adjustments?

If you have accomplished your goal, you should feel good about yourself! Congratulations!

If you haven't, commit to trying again. Perhaps you need to adjust the amount or the schedule. Whatever you do—don't stop completely! You can do this!

Budget

Creating a budget is your starting point. Having a budget is extremely important. It doesn't have to be perfect. It doesn't have to be down to the penny. But, it does have to be . . . meaning it should exist.

It is your budget. Your budget should be created so that it feels right for you. There are a lot of tools available to help you craft your budget. For example, you can use Excel or a notebook. It just has to work *for you.*

A budget should objectively show you where your money goes. It is not about judgement. It is about defining where and how much of your hard-earned money goes to each category.

There are going to be regularly occurring monthly expenses, like mortgage or rent payments, utilities, and buying food. There are also going to be expenses that do not occur every month, but you still must take them into account. For instance, you may get a haircut every other month or spend more on gifts during the holidays.

No one is going to critique your budget. This is for your eyes and your well-being. If you'd like to group items together, that is fine. You may want to have a category called "Entertainment," which you feel should include dining out. Or, maybe you want "Dining Out" as its own category. Perhaps you feel a "Miscellaneous" category would suit your needs. There is no right or wrong way to label your categories or create your budget. What matters is that you capture the expenses. As time goes on, you can always modify your budget.

You can't realistically take ownership of your financial health if you don't have the facts.

<u>Money Movement Plan</u>

You guessed it . . . *create a budget.*

Start by writing down the areas where you think your money goes.

I've provided an example of a variety of budget categories. You can modify it to your specific situation. Add / remove / rename categories as you see fit.

If you want a reality check, the first time you create your budget make an "Estimated Budget." Fill in the corresponding boxes with what you *think* you spend.

After that, create your "Actual Budget" with what you've really spent. Then compare the two. It's usually eye opening.

Referring to credit card and bank statements during this process might help to fill in the blanks.

Once you have completed your spreadsheet, consider the following questions:

- Does anything surprise you?
- Are you spending more (or less) than you thought you were spending?
- In which area(s) are you spending more than you thought?

The big questions:

- Is your income covering your expenses?
- Are you living comfortably?
- Are you able to save money?
- Do adjustments need to be made to your budget?

Budget

	Jan	Feb	Mar	Apr	May	Jun	Jul	Aug	Sept	Oct	Nov	Dec
Mortgage or Rent												
House Tax												
Home Insurance												
Car Tax												
Car Insurance												
Car Payments												
Car Maintenance												
Health Insurance												
Medications												
Water												
Home Phone												
Cell Phone												
Internet / Cable												
Streaming Services												
Electricity												
Heating												
Trash Collection												
Food (Groceries)												
Gas / Commuting												
Clothing												
Entertainment												
Gifts												
Personal Care												
Pets												
Miscellaneous												
Gym Membership												
Savings (Regular)												
Retirement Savings												
Student Loan Debt												
Credit Card Debt												

Care

Care about your financial well-being!
No one else will care as much.

As with other aspects of life, it is important to take care of yourself.

Not only do the majority of Americans not have enough savings to ride out financial hardships, but almost two-thirds won't have enough for retirement (Dennison, 2019). While the Great Recession happened just over a decade ago, a worldwide pandemic began in 2020. As of this writing in early 2021, the pandemic is still in full force. It has been reported that many people's emergency savings have been depleted during this time (Morad, 2021). These are two major events in a pretty short time span. Both have had, and are still having, real consequences on people's lives, including financial ramifications.

Uncertainty is a part of life. While I imagine we all hope for the best, we know that things don't always turn out the way we plan. We can't predict the future. What we can do is prepare as best we can. While you may feel sympathetic towards a neighbor who has lost his job, you probably won't lose sleep over it. However, if you are the one who has suffered the job loss, you will most likely be anxious. Unexpected change and uncertainty tend to have that effect.

To prepare for unexpected events, both big and small, having extra money tucked away is important. You are the author of your story. To ride out those storms, provisions must be made.

If you knew a severe snowstorm was coming, you most likely would stock up on food, maybe get some batteries for your flashlights, and/or have a snow shovel at the ready. Unlike the weather, we do not have a means to forecast the hardships in life. So, the best that we can do is to prepare. That is why having savings set aside is so important. It can help you withstand the financial storms.

Too many people live paycheck to paycheck. This is something that can be addressed. You may have to make changes to your budget, but it is important to know that this can be remedied. There is hope!

While "Care" is the primary word chosen for the letter C, there are other words that need recognition.

Check your account balances on a regular basis. Establishing a routine will help you feel comfortable. Numbers don't lie. If your bank account shows you have $100 balance, it is an indisputable fact. Also, routinely checking your account will help you catch any fraudulent activity quickly.

Caring also extends to others. Don't forget to be charitable! If you are able to help someone else, there are many organizations that can use some assistance. You can donate to scientific research for medical diseases, organizations that help animals, and organizations to help those that have fallen on hard times, just to name a few. In addition to the amazing emotional boost you get from donating, many donations are tax deductible and can keep you from paying more taxes than necessary (9 Positive Effects, 2015).

Also, a donation does not have to be financial. You can donate your time.

Another C phrase that many Americans are familiar with is Credit Cards. Credit cards were introduced in the 1950s (Complete History Of, 2020). That's less than a century ago. To give you a frame of reference, the following things were also created in the 1950s: Superglue, television remote, hula hoops, the polio vaccine, and Barbie dolls (Here's a List, n.d.). The 1950s also gave us Tom Hanks, Denzel Washington, and Katey Sagal (Chaktrovorty, n.d.). Not that old, right? Yet, nearly half of U.S. adults have credit card debt (Horch, 2020).

Paying what you owe goes beyond just paying back credit card debt. Individuals receive credit scores. Your credit score can affect loan rates and insurance rates. It can have an impact on a potential landlord deciding if he would like to rent to you, and employers can also ask to check your credit history (DeNicola, 2020). Your credit score reflects how responsible you are with your money.

If you have credit card debt, again, this is something that you can tackle. If you have multiple credit cards, start by paying down the ones with the highest interest rates first.

Money Movement Plan

Name one thing you currently do that shows you care about your finances. For example,

- Do you know how much your expenses are for the current month?
- Do you know exactly how much you have in your retirement account?
- Do you pay your bills on time each month to avoid unnecessary penalties?

D

Debt

There are going to be times when you need to borrow money, like if you want to own a home or buy a car, or to further your education. Keep a handle on how much debt you have and how much you can comfortably afford.

Interest is charged on every loan. How much more will things cost in the end if you are paying interest?

Question: Do you know how much a $100,000 mortgage will actually cost you at a 4% fixed interest rate over a 30-year period (assuming there is no down payment)?

Answer: A $100,000 mortgage at a 4% fixed interest rate over 30 years will cost you

$171,869.51!

Here's the breakdown:

- $100,000 is your principal (your loan) and
- **$71,869.51 is the interest**.

Using the Bankrate.com amortization calculator and an amortization schedule, here's an abbreviated version of what the breakdown looks like:

Start Date: 1/1/2021
Estimated Payoff Date: 1/1/2051

Amortization Schedule:

Payment Date	Payment	Principal	Interest	Total Interest	Balance
Feb., 2021	$477.42	$144.08	$333.33	$333.33	$99,855.92
Mar., 2021	$477.42	$144.56	$332.85	$666.19	$99,711.36
Apr., 2021	$477.42	$145.04	$332.47	$998.56	$99,566.31
May, 2021	$477.42	$145.53	$331.89	$1,330.45	$99,420.78
Jun., 2021	$477.42	$146.01	$331.40	$1,661.85	$99,274.77
Jul., 2021	$477.42	$146.50	$330.92	$1,992.76	$99,128.27
Aug., 2021	$477.42	$146.99	$330.43	$2,323.19	$98,981.28
Sept., 2021	$477.42	$147.48	$329.94	$2,653.13	$98,833.81
Oct., 2021	$477.42	$147.97	$329.45	$2,982.58	$98,685.84
Nov., 2021	$477.42	$148.46	$328.95	$3,311.53	$98,537.37
Dec., 2021	$477.42	$148.96	$328.46	$3,639.99	$98,388.42
Jan., 2022	$477.42	$149.45	$327.96	$3,967.95	$98,238.96
Jan., 2023	$477.42	$155.54	$321.87	$7,864.15	$96,406.18
Jan., 2024	$477.42	$161.88	$315.54	$11,685.68	$94,498.73
Jan., 2025	$477.42	$168.48	$308.94	$15,429.49	$92,513.56
Jan., 2026	$477.42	$175.34	$302.08	$19,092.43	$90,447.51
Jan., 2027	$477.42	$182.48	$294.93	$22,671.19	$88,297.29

Payment Date	Payment	Principal	Interest	Total Interest	Balance
Jan., 2028	$477.42	$189.92	$287.50	$26,162.36	$86,059.47
Jan., 2029	$477.42	$197.65	$279.76	$29,562.34	$83,730.48
Jan., 2030	$477.42	$205.71	$271.71	$32,867.45	$81,306.59
Jan., 2031	$477.42	$214.09	$263.33	$36,073.79	$78,783.96
Jan., 2032	$477.42	$222.81	$254.60	$39,177.37	$76,158.55
Jan., 2033	$477.42	$231.89	$245.53	$42,173.98	$73,426.17
Jan., 2034	$477.42	$241.34	$236.08	$45,059.27	$70,582.48
Jan., 2035	$477.42	$251.17	$226.25	$47,828.70	$67,622.93
Jan., 2036	$477.42	$261.40	$216.01	$50,477.55	$64,542.80
Jan., 2037	$477.42	$272.05	$205.36	$53,000.92	$61,337.18
Jan., 2038	$477.42	$283.13	$194.28	$55,393.68	$58,000.96
Jan., 2039	$477.42	$294.67	$182.74	$57,650.52	$54,528.82
Jan., 2040	$477.42	$306.68	$170.74	$59,765.91	$50,915.22
Jan., 2041	$477.42	$319.17	$158.25	$61,734.06	$47,154.39
Jan., 2042	$477.42	$332.17	$145.24	$63,549.00	$43,240.34
Jan., 2043	$477.42	$345.71	$131.71	$65,204.47	$39,166.83
Jan., 2044	$477.42	$359.79	$117.62	$66,693.98	$34,927.36
Jan., 2045	$477.42	$374.45	$102.97	$68,010.77	$30,515.16

Payment Date	Payment	Principal	Interest	Total Interest	Balance
Jan., 2046	$477.42	$389.71	$87.71	$69,147.79	$25,923.21
Jan., 2047	$477.42	$405.58	$71.83	$70,097.74	$21,144.17
Jan., 2048	$477.42	$422.11	$55.31	$70,852.98	$16,170.42
Jan., 2049	$477.42	$439.30	$38.11	$71,405.58	$10,994.04
Jan., 2050	$477.42	$457.20	$20.21	$71,747.29	$5,606.76
Jan., 2051	$477.42	$475.83	$1.59	$71,869.51	$0.00

Note: Amortization is when you pay off debt over time in equal installments. Part of each payment goes toward the principal amount of your loan, and part goes towards the interest.

Reviewing an amortization schedule is a sobering look at how much money goes towards interest. You will notice that even though your payments are the same every month, most of your payment goes towards interest at the beginning of your loan.

Payment Date	Payment	Principal	Interest	Total Interest	Balance
Feb., 2021	$477.42	$144.08	**$333.33**	$333.33	$99,855.92
Mar., 2021	$477.42	$144.56	**$332.85**	$666.19	$99,711.36
Apr., 2021	$477.42	$145.04	**$332.47**	$998.56	$99,566.31
May, 2021	$477.42	$145.53	**$331.89**	$1,330.45	$99,420.78
Jun., 2021	$477.42	$146.01	**$331.40**	$1,661.85	$99,274.77
Jul., 2021	$477.42	$146.50	**$330.92**	$1,992.76	$99,128.27

As time goes on, less goes towards your interest, and more goes towards your principal (or your loan) amount.

Payment Date	Payment	Principal	Interest	Total Interest	Balance
Jan., 2046	$477.42	**$389.71**	$87.71	$69,147.79	$25,923.21
Jan., 2047	$477.42	**$405.58**	$71.83	$70,097.74	$21,144.17

Payment Date	Payment	Principal	Interest	Total Interest	Balance
Jan., 2048	$477.42	**$422.11**	$55.31	$70,852.98	$16,170.42
Jan., 2049	$477.42	**$439.30**	$38.11	$71,405.58	$10,994.04
Jan., 2050	$477.42	**$457.20**	$20.21	$71,747.29	$5,606.76
Jan., 2051	$477.42	**$475.83**	$1.59	$71,869.51	$0.00

The good news is that you can reduce the amount of interest you pay in the end if you can make additional payments. For example, many Americans get a tax refund when filing their taxes for the year. Using the same $100,000 loan example above, if you added an additional $1,000 payment *each year* towards your mortgage, you could pay it off a minimum of seven years sooner **and** save around $20,000 in interest that would have gone to the bank.

Source: Bankrate.com

Here's what the amortization schedule looks like towards the end of your loan when you add the extra yearly payment.

Payment Date	Payment	Principal	Interest	Total Interest	Balance
Mar., 2042	$477.42	$445.46	$31.95	$51,403.64	$9,140.16
Apr., 2042	**$1,477.42**	**$1,446.95**	$30.47	$51,434.11	$7,693.21
May, 2042	$477.42	$451.77	$25.64	$51,459.75	$7,241.44
Jun., 2042	$477.42	$453.28	$24.14	$51,483.89	$6,788.16
Jul., 2042	$477.42	$453.28	$22.63	$51,506.52	$6,333.37
Aug., 2042	$477.42	$456.30	$21.11	$51,527.63	$5,877.07
Sept., 2042	$477.42	$457.83	$19.59	$51,547.22	$5,419.24
Oct., 2042	$477.42	$459.35	$18.06	$51,565.28	$4,959.89
Nov., 2042	$477.42	$460.88	$16.53	$51,581.82	$4,499.01
Dec., 2042	$477.42	$462.42	$15.00	$51,596.81	$4,036.59
Jan., 2043	$477.42	$463.96	$13.46	$51,610.27	$3,572.63
Feb., 2043	$477.42	$465.51	$11.91	$51,622.18	$3,107.12
Mar., 2043	$477.42	$467.06	$10.36	$51,632.53	$2,640.06
Apr., 2043	**$1,477.42**	**$1,468.62**	$8.80	$51,641.33	$1,171.45
May, 2043	$477.42	$473.51	$3.90	$51,645.24	$697.94
Jun., 2043	$477.42	$475.09	$2.33	$51,647.57	$222.85
Jul., 2043	$223.59	$222.85	$0.74	$51,648.31	$0.00

In sports terminology, it's better to play offense than defense. In financial terminology, this translates to *it's better to save money in advance than paying interest on your debt.*

Now, let's look at another scenario.

If you are planning to purchase a home for $100,000 and you have a 20% down payment, or $20,000, then you will be asking the bank for an $80,000 mortgage. Assuming the same 4% fixed interest rate over a 30-year period, this will bring your monthly payment down to $381.93. Your total interest paid over the 30-year period will amount to $57,495.61.

If you add additional yearly payments of $1,000, just as we had in our previous example, you can achieve almost another $19,000 of savings on what you would have paid in interest.

Money Movement Plan

If you have debt, use an online amortization calculator and review the amortization schedule to see how much you will end up paying in interest.

- Do you think you can make an extra yearly payment towards the principal amount of your loan?
- Would you rather make an extra monthly payment towards the principal amount of your loan?

Here are a few examples of how you can make an extra payment towards debt and how to deal with debt.

Example #1:

Your take-home pay is $800 every two weeks. This means you would receive 26 paychecks for the calendar year (52 weeks in a year divided by two since you're paid biweekly). If you structure your budget to rely on two paychecks per month, multiply that by 12 months, the total is 24. The two paychecks that you haven't accounted for in your budget can now go as an extra payment towards the principal amount of your debt.

Or maybe you get a paycheck once a month. Add an extra payment into your figures based on your frequency of income. If you've already accounted for an extra payment, it should make it easier to follow through.

Example #2:

If you have already allotted enough money to each budget category, and let's say you find yourself with an extra $100 at the end of each month, if the interest rate on your debt exceeds the interest rate on any of your savings / investments, you can put the extra money toward the principal amount of your debt.

Example #3:

Put a lump sum towards the principal amount of your debt. Many individuals get a yearly tax return. This would be an easy way to work on paying down your debt without taking away from your normal monthly budget.

Example #4:

Perhaps you've gotten a second job for the specific purpose of paying down debt. It's additional income and a great way to tackle tough financial problems.

Example #5:

Live below your means. If your home is a little smaller, your bills will be too. If your college is a public university versus a private university, you can better manage your debt; there will be less of it to manage. You get the idea.

Example #6:

As you get raises at work, consider using the additional income towards multiple goals. For example, a 3% raise could mean an extra 1% towards paying down credit card debt, 1% towards paying a little extra on the principal of your mortgage or student loan debt, and an extra 1% towards saving a little more for retirement. Dividing your newfound money among different budget categories is a plan that could leave you feeling good. And, it's a relatively painless way to address financial headaches since it's money you didn't have before.

Example #7:

Don't take on more debt than you can handle to begin with.

Expenses

Expenses are bills that need to be paid and purchases that are your responsibility.

You are responsible for your financial well-being.

You're responsible for creating it.

You're responsible for fixing it, if need be.

Can you name four things you see in this room that would prompt a recurring expense?

Answer:

1. Water from the faucet

2. Food in the fridge and on the counter

3. Electricity to run lights and appliances

4. Heat that is programmed through the thermostat on the wall

While "Expenses" is the primary word chosen for the letter E, there are other words that we should talk about.

Unexpected expenses can happen. Emergencies can and do happen! Establishing an "Emergency Fund" is imperative. If you think there is no wiggle room in your budget to put money aside for an "Emergency Fund," this is a good time to examine *wants* and *needs*. It is worth removing a little money in your budget for "wants" so that you can better prepare for emergencies. Could you give up buying coffee for a few days a week? Do you subscribe to multiple streaming services but don't use them all? Do you use enough data on your cell phone plan to merit the unlimited plan? Could you reduce that bill by monitoring your data usage? Do you still mail checks to pay bills? You can save postage and time by setting up electronic payments through your bank. Every little bit helps. Your choices add up . . . literally. There is no better time than now to review your budget and determine if you're putting your money in the right places. Having extra money put aside is essential. It is the foundation, or base, to your financial building blocks.

Speaking of extra money . . . are you living paycheck to paycheck?

If you don't have any extra money at the end of each month, you <u>must</u> evaluate your situation. Again, start by looking at your expenses (*wants vs needs*) to see if there's anything you can cut. Some financial situations may require you to consider getting a second job or possibly downsizing your home.

Living paycheck to paycheck is a stressful situation that can be addressed. You need to figure out how to increase or free up money, and then implement the plan.

Money Movement Plan

Get a pad and paper. Sit down in your favorite place in your home. Look around and list the things in that room. For example, if you're in the living room, you probably have a couch, lamps, tables, a television, etc. Now, put a dollar figure next to each item. How much did you pay for each piece? When you're done, calculate the total of your list. How much did you spend on all the things in that room?

Now, take that total and divide by your hourly wage. So, for example, if you have $500 worth of items on your list and you get paid $15 an hour, that will mean you would have had to have worked over 33 hours to furnish the items in your chosen room.

Fixed Expenses

Fixed Expenses are bills that stay consistent. Try to get the best rates you can, where you can, so your costs will remain steady and comfortable.

	Insurance	Rent	Internet	Streaming Services
January	$100	$800	$60	$10
February	$100	$800	$60	$10
March	$100	$800	$60	$10
April	$100	$800	$60	$10
May	$100	$800	$60	$10

Fixed Expenses can reduce Fear

Yes, fear is a four-letter F word.

Fear can stop you from doing the things you should be doing to give yourself a better chance at security.

If you fear your finances, you might avoid them. And avoidance won't solve any financial problems.

You may be a person who fears their finances:

- If your partner handles all the finances and you aren't in the loop.
- If you don't know your numbers: how much you have, how much you owe, when bills are due, and how much your interest rates are on your debt.
- If you don't want to open billing statements because you don't want to know what it says.
- If you don't want to open retirement savings statements because you don't think you are saving enough for retirement.
- If you open another credit card and shift your balance to the new card rather than dealing with the debt you already have on your existing credit cards.

If you are grappling with finance-based fear, for any reason, liberate yourself with facts. Facing the reality of your finances is the first step. Confront your fears. If, for example, you have $10,000 of credit card debt, you now know what you're dealing with. You have acknowledged and named the fear. The fear is $10,000 worth of debt. Next, you can create a plan to pay down your debt, and by doing so, you can work towards overcoming your fear.

Bring the truth to light. The light will extinguish the fear.

Fight is a word not many people talk about as it relates to money issues. Yet, fighting about money is common. It's one of the biggest things couples fight about. It's said to be the number one reason for divorce (Barrett, 2018). People have also lost friends over borrowed money not being repaid. Families can fight over inheritances.

In addition, much of modern politics boils down to differences over how to handle finances: what programs to fund, how much to tax employees, how much to tax employers, how much to tax residents of a town, where taxpayers money goes, whether there's a shortage in a government budget, when it's appropriate to tax, when it's not appropriate to tax, whether to give tax breaks to corporations, etc. Yet, I don't really hear constituents ask political candidates if they know how to manage money. Why aren't candidates asked what they would do if they couldn't make ends meet on a government level? Front and center on today's political stage are conversations of ideals and values. That's great, but where are the difficult conversations about money?

To give you an example, the state I currently live in was facing a budget shortfall. So, I took a quick look at the state budget (Capital Budget, n.d.). In my brief examination, one of the things I discovered was that there was money designated for renovations. Now, if you're facing a shortfall, there should be no renovations in your budget until you are financially equipped to handle them. Just as individuals must define what is a *need* and what is a *want*, our politicians should be viewing a budget the same way and prioritizing accordingly. After all, according to *The Gettysburg Address*, the government is of, by, and for the people. If we all put forth the necessary effort to make reasonable financial choices, I'm convinced there would be less fighting. Peace is a great reason to strive for better financial management.

Money Movement Plan

What is your biggest money fear?

- Create a plan to deal with it. If you're not at the point where you're ready to implement a plan, think about ways to make your financial fear less scary.

For example, maybe you are afraid you won't be able to afford a house. An alternative is to rent a home. Weigh the pros and cons of owning a house. You may feel differently once you see there are benefits to renting. If your goal is to purchase a home, you can set a timeline and determine a more realistic timeframe for when you would be able to afford a house. Your goal would still be within reach, and you will be better prepared when it's time to make the move.

Your options may not be ideal, but they should be realistic and make you feel less anxious. In the meantime, you can still find other ways to address the issue like attempting to save more money by trying to get a job with a higher income or working overtime, if that's an option.

Another tip: To manage the fear and to avoid worrying about money 24/7, schedule time each week to check in on your financial health. It should be a minimum of once per week. Then your brain can relax because it will know there is a set time for money matters.

Goals

Think about the goals you have for your life.

Are your goals realistic?

Are your goals what you really want, or is it something you believe that you should want?

How long will it take to achieve each goal? How much will each goal cost?

It's good to have goals!

Here is an example of a realistic goal versus a nonrealistic goal:

Peter is in high school. He's working a part-time job after school. He feels like not having a mode of transportation is affecting his life. He has to depend on someone else for a ride to work. He's not able to go to the baseball field to play a spontaneous game with his friends. So, Peter's goal is to buy a car within a year.

An unrealistic goal would be for Peter to purchase a new car. Given his status as a full-time student along with the fact that he is a part-time, low-paid employee, it's not feasible for Peter to buy a new car. The car salesman might be very persuasive and promise flexible financing options, but this would not be a financially responsible or realistic goal for Peter.

Given his situation and the time frame of his goal, a used car would be in Peter's best interest. Even if Peter can't afford to buy a car outright, saving as much as he can for a down payment will be a big help. If he doesn't want a loan, he may have to choose a car that doesn't meet all his expectations. It may not have a navigation system or an incredible stereo. That's ok! If Peter plans well, down the road he will have more options available to him.

Often, we get comfortable with the way our parents or caregivers have been providing for us. However, it's important to know that every adult has had to work their way up the economic ladder. You can afford more when you make more.

What Peter also has to understand is there are more costs associated with having a car:

- Gas

- Car insurance
- Car maintenance
- A driver's license
- Car registration
- Emissions testing

Goals should be realistic. You should establish a time frame. Will it affect your ability to attain other goals? Maybe Peter wants a car, and he wants to take a trip in the summer. Can he do both? Before making any big purchases, ask yourself if it's something you really want and if it will make reaching another goal harder in the long run.

Money Movement Plan

Reflect on your goals:

- What's your biggest goal at the moment? Come up with a realistic plan, within a realistic time frame, for how you're going to achieve your goal.
- Define your short-term and long-term goals. For example, taking a vacation this summer is a short-term goal. If retirement is a long way off, saving for retirement is a long-term goal.

SMART goals can be a helpful tool in this exercise. SMART is an acronym for Specific, Measurable, Attainable, Realistic, Timely. Using the SMART formula can help you put together a solid plan (SMART goal, 2015).

People usually have multiple goals. Again, it's good to have goals!

> **"You are never too old to set another goal or to dream a new dream."**
> **C. S. Lewis**

Happiness

When you hear the words "money and happiness", what comes to mind? Is it a philosophical question? An old proverb says, "money can't buy happiness". No amount of money can give you the feeling of love: love of a parent, a spouse, a child, a friend, a pet. Perhaps you'd categorize the coupling of money and happiness as a practical imperative. After all, it's hard to imagine being comfortable in present times without money. Would you be happy on a cold winter's night if you didn't have a roof over your head or heat to keep you warm?

I propose the perspective that money is pragmatic. It is a tool. If money and happiness are to go hand in hand, use money as the means to achieve your goals of comfort, security, and yes, sometimes fun.

Advertisements are infused into every aspect of life. In this world of consumerism, what money means on a personal level has become hazy.

Are your choices helping you to feel happy and financially secure?

One of the worst ways to find happiness and security is to compare yourself to others. Keep your mind and your heart on your own situation. Don't waste your time or your money trying to be like someone else. Live your own authentic life. Be yourself. Do what's best for your situation. **Live your best financial life.**

Making good choices can result in having financial stability and can help you sleep better at night. It's one less thing to worry about ... one *very* big thing.

Happiness is in the ability to keep a roof over your head and put food on the table.

Happiness is being content with what you have and not feeling a need for more.

Happiness can be had knowing that potential emergencies will be cushioned by savings you've diligently and purposefully set aside.

Happiness can be had when you're debt free. It can provide peace, a sense of freedom, and accomplishment.

Happiness is achieving goals you've set for yourself to make your life a little easier and perhaps give you the luxury of choice.

Happiness is finding joy in saving for the future.

Happiness is spending less when you could easily spend more.

Happiness is getting a deal on something, allowing you to make a purchase while saving a few bucks.

Happiness is *making* something versus *buying* something. Putting your heart into a creation is so much more rewarding than putting your money into it.

If you haven't reached your goals, be happy knowing that you're doing the best you can. You only fail if you don't try.

Even if money is tight, you can achieve happiness. There may be difficult decisions to be made but taking steps towards financial independence is what's needed. Get organized, make a plan, look at your options, and prioritize what's important.

Money Movement Plan

While it is important to assess your overall happiness, this plan focuses on financial happiness:

- Do something small that will lead to financial happiness. For example, if you're grocery shopping for the week, plan your meals around food that's on sale. You can also clip coupons. If paper coupons aren't your thing, there are digital coupons.
- Set a goal for yourself. If your goal is to save an extra $5 this week, then strive for that goal and continue for a month.
- It's not always about the big wins. The little wins will add up too. An extra $5 a week of savings will add up to $260 for the year.
- Name one thing that makes you happy that's not related to money.
- Know that having money doesn't guarantee happiness. It can provide comfort and stability, but it isn't everything.

Income

There are three ways to make a budget work:

1. Increase your income
2. Cut your expenses
3. A combination of increasing your income and cutting your expenses.

Making a budget work is not a secret only given to a select group of privileged people. Like many things, it's what you do with that knowledge that is important. Remember, if you do nothing, then nothing will change.

Even with this simple, boiled down, summary version of how to make a budget work, many people focus on the expenses and not the income.

Income is money received either through working or a return on an investment.

There are no shortcuts. Work hard and try to make good decisions.

In today's modern world of remote work and internet opportunities, it's more accessible than ever to find an additional source of income. Having a second stream of income is not uncommon. If you're a teacher, you can tutor. If you're creative, you can sell your wares online. You can perform administrative tasks in a work from home job. The list goes on. There are opportunities if you need it, or if you just want to do it for fun or a little extra cash. For example, having a full-time corporate job can be offset with the creativity of making products you sell online. It's an option. You may have a passive income, which is money that comes in with little to no effort to maintain. This can be renting out an apartment, creating an app, or receiving dividends from an investment, just to name a few examples.

Speaking of Investments ...

There are different kinds of investments. Stocks, mutual funds, bonds, Certificates of Deposit, Exchange Traded Funds, annuities, and real estate are some different types of investments.

Whatever you choose to invest in, if you choose to invest, always:

> 1. Do your homework, and
> 2. Figure out your risk tolerance

If something feels too risky for your liking, then don't do it. Figuring out your risk tolerance means finding what level of risk you're comfortable with. If you don't like taking risks, then you are risk averse and may want to stick with more stable investments.

It's worth mentioning that for nearly the last century, the historical average stock market return has been 10% (Royal, 2020). The stock market fluctuates. It is not a guaranteed return on investment. But again, research your investment choices and decide on what you're comfortable with.

If you're considering a mutual fund, exchange traded funds (ETFs), or any other fund, look at the expense ratio associated with the fund. This fee covers expenses such as management fees, administrative fees, operating costs, and all other expenses (Account Summary, n.d.). A lower expense ratio is beneficial to you as an investor because less money is going towards expenses.

Also, if you are considering a fund of some sort or an individual stock, look at ones that pay dividends. The definition of a dividend is when a company pays out a portion of its profits to the company's shareholders (Dividend, 2021). If the company or fund you invest in provides dividends, it's additional income.

You can also decide if you'd like to reinvest your dividends. This can be a beneficial investment strategy. I'll try to show you what this means in the following example.

Let's say you buy 100 shares of Stock A at $10 a share. You've spent $1000 for Stock A. Now, let's say that Stock A provides a 2.5% dividend yield. A dividend yield is the amount of money a company pays shareholders for owning a share of its stock divided by its current stock price (Fernando, 2021). In this example, it means an additional $25 beyond your original investment in the stock.

If the stock remains at $10, you can purchase another two and a half shares of Stock A if you've elected to reinvest your dividends.

Fast forward a year. Stock A is now $12 a share. Not only has your investment increased by 20% on the price of the stock alone, but now you own more shares. So, instead of $12 per share times 100 shares, it's now $12 times 102.5 shares. You've made $1,230 versus $1,200 if you sell all 102.5 shares at the $12 price.

Still sticking with this example, let's change the scenario a bit.

You buy 100 shares of Stock A at $10 a share. You've spent $1000 for Stock A.
Stock A provides a 2.5% dividend yield. That's an additional $25 beyond your original investment in the stock.

If the stock remains at $10, you can purchase another two and a half shares of Stock A if you've elected to reinvest your dividends.

Fast forward a year. Stock A is now $8 a share. If you've elected to reinvest your dividends, assuming the dividend yield is still at 2.5%, you can now buy even more shares because the price of the stock is lower. At the $8 stock price, $25 would allow you to buy an additional 3.125 shares.

If Stock A goes back to $10 a share at some point, then you have 103.125 shares available to sell.

Note: None of the examples presented take tax considerations into account.

Another important consideration related to investments is your age. Time is a factor. If you are younger and a risky investment turns out poorly, you have more time to recover from potential losses. However, if you are older and need that investment money for your retirement, then a riskier investment is probably a bad idea.

Money Movement Plan

Thinking of your own personal situation, if you needed an extra $1000 by the end of the month, how would you approach the problem?

- Cut expenses where possible?
- Sell your car and take the bus?
- Take on an extra job or increase your hours at work?
- Downsize your home?
- Eat meals from your food storage?

Jackpot

Few people win the lottery. Wishing, hoping, and dreaming are not actual plans. So, make a real plan!

To honor the "jackpot" theme, as well as to keep with the Js, the following section is entitled "Joke or No Joke". It is money-related trivia where your answer should reflect whether you think it's a joke (meaning it's false) or if it's no joke (meaning the answer is true).

Here we go!

Joke or No Joke?

1. The motto on the first U.S. coin was "Mind Your Business."
2. The U.S. Secret Service was established to protect the American president.
3. There have been women on U.S. paper currency.
4. 30% of the world's currency is physical money.
5. Living presidents can be portrayed on U.S. currency.
6. TSA collected almost a million dollars in loose change in 2018.
7. Some people bury pennies in the garden to deter snails.
8. There are secret designs on the $1 bill.

Answers to "Joke or No Joke"

1. *No Joke* - "Mind Your Business" was on the first one cent "Fugio" coin. The coin was designed by Benjamin Franklin in 1787.
2. *Joke* - The U.S. Secret Service was established in 1865 to fight counterfeiting.
3. *No Joke* - Pocahontas appeared on the $20 bill during the 1860s and Martha Washington was on $1 silver certificates in 1886 and in the 1890s.
4. *Joke* - Around 90% of the world's currency is digital.
5. *Joke* - Congress issued a law in 1866 stating that no living person can be portrayed on American currency.
6. *No Joke* - TSA claimed nearly a million dollars in loose change in 2018 and 2019:
     - 2018: $960,105.49 (Travelers leave behind, n.d.).
     - 2019: $926,030.44 (Passengers left more, 2020).
7. *No Joke* - Some people bury pennies in the garden because it's said that the slugs will get an electric shock from the copper and zinc in pennies.
8. *No Joke* - There are designs on the $1 bill that relate to the original 13 colonies. For example, there are 13 steps on the pyramid, 13 stars above the eagle, and 13 berries on the olive branch in one of the eagle's talons.

Know Your Numbers

Numbers are reality! You'll be better equipped to make good choices if you know what you're working with.

HONESTY is key! Be honest with yourself about your finances.

From the section on budgeting, I stated that you can't realistically take ownership of your financial health if you don't have the facts. It's worth repeating.

You can't successfully respond to issues if you are missing information or if your information is inaccurate. You can't make good decisions based on bad data.

Another K word is keep.

- *Keep focused.* Stay on top of your accounts, your debt, your budget, and your goals. Remind yourself what you're working towards and why.
- If you stumble while trying to get yourself on track, *keep trying.* Sometimes it takes a little time to find your way.
- *Keep learning.* There are many ways to continue to grow. Many colleges offer online classes to continue your education. Not only will it keep you sharp, but you may learn a new skill that is marketable and can help with income, or you could learn a new skill like knitting. Some town libraries offer classes on different subjects, like expanding your knowledge on Microsoft Excel. Also, continuing to learn about money-related topics should give you an advantage when dealing with your own finances. For example, if you learn that a bank has a lower interest rate on mortgages, you may consider refinancing your own mortgage.
- *Keep up the good work.* If you've found what works for you in tackling your financial problems, *keep at it!* Finances are an everyday issue.
- *Keep going.* Even if you meet your goals, continue with what's been working for you.

If you have eight months of savings set aside for emergencies, wouldn't a year's worth of savings give you a little more comfort? There's no reason to spend your hard-earned money foolishly just because you've hit your mark. Continue with those good habits.

Money Movement Plan

Demonstrate your knowledge related to something you're good at. For example, maybe you have a hobby and can share your expertise with someone who wants to learn, or you can write down a recipe for something you cook that everyone loves.

When you find a way to relay your knowledge, ask yourself how you can apply it to a financial subject. For example, if you have recently researched colleges, you can make a chart of the different schools you're interested in and list the pros and cons of each school. There should be a financial element to this activity. So, in this example, you may make a chart which shows the price of an in-state school and out-of-state school, with a further breakdown of costs for tuition, room and board, and textbooks. Assuming there is an out-of-state school on your list, add travel costs for returning home, and multiply it by how many times you think you will visit home during the school year.

The idea behind this activity is not only to be knowledgeable in a subject, but also to feel comfortable providing an explanation, which would mean you should feel comfortable in the understanding of the topic you've chosen. It should give you confidence.

Live Below, or at Least Within, Your Means

Big purchases, like a home or a car, can mean big bills. Deciding how and where to further your education can add to debt, but it is an investment in yourself and your future. **These kinds of decisions can set the tone for years to come.**

One of the best ways to gain financial independence is to make smart decisions at the outset. Knowing your boundaries is a great start. To illustrate a way to live within your means, consider one of the biggest purchases people make today: a home. If you know how much house you can afford, you can figure out how to stay within your limits. The smaller your purchase, the less debt you take on. Don't forget the related bills that go with it. A bigger house can mean more taxes and more spent on utilities, like your heating bill because you're heating a larger space, etc. There also tends to be more maintenance and home decor purchases to fill the space. If you purchase a smaller house, a cheaper car, or decide to attend a less expensive college, you could be putting more of your savings towards other things like retirement or vacations. Something else to remember: try to get good interest rates on both savings and debt.

A bigger house won't necessarily make you happier. A used car will still get you from Point A to Point B. In fact, not stretching yourself thin can lead to less stress.

When you're making a big financial purchase, figure out what's important to you. You can make a list. Decide where you are willing to compromise and where you are not.

As a case in point, Patrick, a twenty-something year old, was searching for a place to live during the housing bubble in the early years of the twenty-first century. He loved the town he grew up in and really wanted to stay there. Although he managed to save a fair amount for a down payment, the price of real estate was going up faster than he could save to keep up with the ongoing trend.

There are several things that were important to him: to live in a nice suburban town, close to family, friends, and work, where he would feel comfortable. He preferred a house but knew the upkeep involved would be an additional expense in the form of both time and money. It was another thing to keep in mind. However, on the other side of the coin, he would be able to make home improvements as he saw fit without being bound by the rules of a condo association if he decided on a condominium in the end.

After realistically reviewing his options, he didn't feel he could comfortably afford a house and all the related expenses that went with it. Patrick looked into condominiums in some neighboring towns. He also considered renting. The fact of the matter was he would have to cover all the bills on his income alone as it would be a sole purchase. He wasn't

splitting the bills with anyone else. Patrick was
determined to be responsible for his decisions.

After doing his research and weighing his options,
Patrick decided on a condominium in a
neighboring town. It met all his important
requirements. It was still within a reasonable
distance from family, friends, and work; it was in a
quaint suburban town; and, in the end, his bills
were lower, and he didn't have to worry about
outdoor upkeep. He was living below his means. All
his compromises were ones he could live with and
still feel happy. The town he chose to reside in
became his new home. It's where he still lives today
and loves it a little more every day.

Once the real estate bubble burst and the Great
Recession set in, like many others, Patrick was out
of work. He was able to stretch his savings further
with lower expenses. It helped him ride out the
financial storm until he was able to find a full-time
job again and get back on his feet.

Your financial decisions literally add up! There is
no need to make rash decisions when you could
take your time and design a well-thought-out plan.

<u>**Money Movement Activity**</u>

How would you approach building a home in a financially responsible way? Here's a way to practice:

- Choose from the components below to build a residence. Assume you have $20,000 for a down payment and you have a 30-year fixed interest rate of 4.5% on a mortgage.

  Hint: use an online mortgage calculator to figure out your mortgage payment.

- Total the dollar amount of your choices.
- Once you've calculated your total, ask yourself if you can comfortably handle the expenses on a salary of $49,000 a year, before taxes.
- If you can't cover the cost of your choices on a $49,000 salary, what compromises are you willing to make?

A. **House A** is selling for $225,000 that has been recently updated and needs minimal work. Yearly taxes are $5,000. It's in a neighborhood with many young families and is within a reasonable distance to major highways.
B. **House B** is a modest house in need of some repair, but no serious updates are needed.

The house is selling for $200,000. Yearly taxes are $4,000. It's in a neighborhood with a mix of families young and old. It is a little further away from major highways but not to the point where it's burdensome.

C. **House C** is a fixer upper that's in need of repairs. Some cosmetic updates would be nice, but it does need a new hot water heater. It also has two broken windows and an eighteen year old refrigerator. The house is selling for $160,000 as is. Yearly taxes are $3,000 before updates are made. The town is planning on reassessing the value of your home next year, so your taxes may go up. It is on a main road in town. It's close to a central shopping center.

D. **Option D** is a two-bedroom condominium. You don't have a private back yard, but it's a newer condo with a good layout and a decent amount of living space. There is also a one-car garage attached to the unit. It's selling for $170,000. Yearly taxes are $3,000. There is also a monthly Homeowner Association (HOA) fee of $300. There is a mix of residents. It's within a reasonable distance to major highways.

E. **Option E** is renting a two-bedroom apartment. It's a one year lease for $1,100 a month. The landlord is requiring a first and last month security deposit. You are not allowed to have pets. It's on the outskirts of town. The apartment does not have a washer or dryer within the unit. You can't make any significant updates to the apartment without approval from the landlord, and it has green carpeting. If the landlord does approve an update, such as replacing the carpet, he will not allow you to deduct the expense from your rent. Annual taxes are the responsibility of the owner. It's within a reasonable distance to major highways and has a small shopping center close by.

F. Replace the flooring this year, which will cost you a total of $1,000.

G. Replace two windows this year, which will cost you a total of $1,500.

H. You want to purchase new lawn furniture for a total of $800.

I. You want to purchase some lawn furniture that will do for now until you can afford something nice. Total is $150.

J. You want to paint some interior rooms yourself for $250.

K. You want to hire painters to paint some interior rooms for $400.

L. You hire someone to mow your lawn over the summer for $300 total.

M. You hire someone to plow your driveway when it snows. They charge $40 per

driveway. It typically snows five to 10 times
per winter in the area.

N. Purchase three major appliances this year
for a total of $2,000. They are lower end to
average models.

O. Purchase three major appliances this year
for a total of $5,000. They are higher-end
models.

M

Meaning

What is the meaning of money?

I'm not going to provide some textbook definition of currency. Instead, I'm going to define what I've perceived as the meaning of money in my experience.

The meaning of money is security. The more you have, the more secure you feel. The less you have, the less secure you feel.

It is a means to an end. If you have enough, you can live comfortably. You can afford things that will make and keep you healthy. You can afford to see a doctor when you are not. It can purchase the essentials and nonessentials. Having an abundance provides comfort, peace of mind, and freedom.

The lack of money can lead to anxiety. Not having the ability to take care of yourself, and perhaps your loved ones, diminishes that feeling of security.

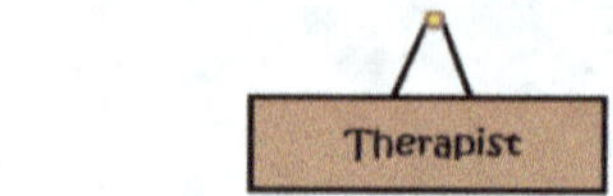

What is your relationship with money?

Money Movement Plan

Reflection: you can answer these questions in your head, but it will be more effective if you write them down.

- Think back to a time when you didn't have enough money for something you either needed or wanted. How did that make you feel?
- Think back to a time when you were able to comfortably afford something you either needed or wanted. How did that make you feel?
- Do you notice any habits or patterns when it comes to your finances? For instance, do you go online shopping when you're under stress? Are you making purchases to compensate for something that's making you emotionally sad?
  Generally speaking, do you avoid dealing with your finances because of something that's based in emotion?
- Give this topic some thought. Understanding underlying habits may lead you to discover why you make the financial choices you make. Getting to the root cause of any issues can help you move forward.

N

Need

When you need something, it's essential. There's a difference between needing and wanting something.

Food is essential. However, dining at restaurants seven times a month is not. You can cook your own meals.

Clothes are essential. However, expensive clothes are not. You don't need a $400 pair of shoes.

You may need a vacation for your mental health, but you don't need to travel to an island to get some rest.

I think most adults understand the difference between **needing** and **wanting** something, so I won't belabor the point. Instead, we can play a Money Movement Game.

Which of the following is NOT a need?

A. Medicine

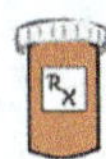

B. The latest smartphone model

C. Food

Answer:

- Medicine is a need.
- Food is a need.
- The latest smartphone model is not.

B is the correct answer.

If you chose anything other than B, you may want to skip ahead to P for Prioritize. 😜

O

Options

An option is when you have the opportunity to make a choice. Knowing what all your options are will help you to make better informed decisions.

Thornton Wilder, an American playwright and novelist, once said "The more decisions that you are forced to make alone, the more you are aware of your freedom to choose."

We make decisions every day. Big ones. Small ones. Ones that seem inconsequential. Ones that seem monumental. Some we feel ill prepared to make. Others feel easy.

You are ultimately responsible for your own financial well-being. The choices that relate to money are very objective. They literally add up.

We can choose quality or the lack thereof, like buying a cheap pair of sneakers that probably won't last long or a more expensive pair that you may get more use out of but might question if it's worth the cost.

We can choose quantity, like buying coffee every day. How much does that habit add up to per year?

We can choose to do nothing at all. Maybe hold off on renovations until you have some money put aside.

We can decide between two options or two hundred options.

We make choices constantly. What are your choices? Do you give much thought to your financial decisions? If you do, when do you think about it?

- *Before*: Do you research a purchase or make a plan?
- *During*: When you take out your credit card, do you give any thought to how much debt is currently on your card?
- *After*: Do you evaluate your spending habits or wonder if you could have gotten a better interest rate at another bank?

It's important to know what all your options are. Again, you can't make good decisions if you don't have all the information. It isn't about choosing the least expensive option. It's about making the right decision for yourself in your current situation.

Money Movement Activity

Consider the following scenario.

Amy wants a new pair of jeans. If you were Amy, which option would you pick?

A
Boyfriend Jeans
$45

B
Flare Jeans
$90

C
Don't buy new jeans because
I already own 15 pairs

Answer:

Whether you chose A, B, or C, there is no incorrect answer. *You can choose whatever you'd like. You are the one who gets to decide what's best and live with the consequences.* If buying something adds to your debt, it's your debt to repay. If you feel like owning sixteen pairs of jeans because it makes you happy, that's your choice. If you can afford a hundred pairs of jeans, and that's what you choose to spend your money on, that's fine too. It's *your financial tale. It's a compilation of choices.*

P

Prioritize

Figure out what's important to you and adjust accordingly!

If you get a paycheck or some kind of defined income, like social security, then you have boundaries. You should be living within the parameters of those boundaries. You have the means to be able to afford a finite number of things. The bigger your income, the more you can afford.

Like most people, you probably have to plan for larger purchases and long-term goals. You have to decide where and how much of your money will go towards future goals.

If you are currently having a hard time living within your means, you may even have to prioritize short-term expenses, like how much money you have to spend on groceries this month.

Money Movement Plan

Identify what's important. List them. Rank them. Prioritize accordingly!

Quantity

How much? How much house do you need? How much will it cost to cover expenses? Do you make enough in income to cover those expenses? If so, do you think you can continue to make enough to cover your expenses and save for the future? How much "stuff" is enough?

Living in a smaller space forces a person to stay on top of their stuff: clothing, furniture, toys, purchases for the home (all purchases in general). It can serve a person well.

There was a point when I was buying storage boxes to store my stuff. I love organization, don't get me wrong, but I had to stop and ask myself: Am I purchasing boxes just to put away something I most likely wouldn't use again? If so, then was that really the best use of my time, space, and money? The answer was no.

There's something to minimalism. If you have less stuff, then you have less to manage. It gives you back more time and space. It also means you're not spending money on something that isn't going to be used and then later potentially having to spend more money to get rid of it. For example, having to hire someone to move a large piece of furniture out of your apartment or spending money on a storage unit. Also, there are environmental benefits of more "stuff" not ending up in landfills.

Sometimes, it doesn't even make sense to buy the stuff you think you need in the first place. As an example, if you own a house and have a lawn, the lawn will need to be mowed. You could buy a lawnmower and pay for gas and maintenance of the lawnmower. We won't even discuss how maintaining a lawn eats into your down time on the weekend. Does it make more sense to hire someone to mow your lawn? Doing so would also free up space in your garage. Only you can decide, once you've done your research.

Compare the cost of owning a lawn mower to lawn mowing services. How often would the grass need to be cut? Do you live in an area where it's seasonal and green grass isn't a year round thing? Lawn mowers have an average life span of 8 - 10 years. You would have to take the cost of replacing it into consideration. If you do hire someone to mow your lawn, you get the added benefit of infusing money back into the local economy.

The point is, it doesn't always make sense financially to accumulate stuff. If you need it or think you will get frequent use out of an item, or if it has sentimental value, then it makes sense. But, if it's something that's going to sit in a box somewhere and not see the light of day, think about donating your things and doing some good in the process by passing it along to someone who could use your donation.

More non-accumulating options include renting tools, tables, and chairs. You can rent bikes, cars, textbooks, fitness gear, and surprisingly, caskets. You can use a nicer casket during the viewing and switch to a less expensive casket for the burial (Howard, 2009). You can still borrow books from the library at no cost, but now you have the additional option of borrowing an eBook. Ok, I may not be fully *"woke"* with respect to everything you can rent . . . yes, it's the casket. But the point is, there are options. You must do your research.

These days there is so much that can be, and is, digitized. We can carry around our music, book, and picture libraries in our smartphones thanks to the cloud. Documents can be scanned. Movies can be queued up on a smart tv. Encyclopedias are a thing of the past thanks to the internet and search engines. Bills and paperwork are commonly emailed. Invoices are often paid online. Even transferring money from individual to individual has made it to the digital age. You can split the lunch check with friends without ever taking out a dollar bill.

I'm not suggesting you live in a sterile environment with no style, but modern technology has provided alternatives.

In the 1980s, bigger was better. Heavy televisions, bulky computers, and big hair. Don't get me wrong--I loved the 80s--especially the music. It had character! But technology, and hair, has been toned down. Many things are far more accessible and with that comes flexibility.

Case in point, I love receiving Christmas cards with pictures of friends and families. Instead of throwing them away once the season is over, you can scan the pictures. Then, you will still have the memories but not another pile of papers.

If you have things that are special to you, like books or pictures, that you want a physical copy of, by all means, display and/or keep what is special. But, if there are things you don't need or want to see on a regular basis, scanning or having a digital copy can be a great option. You don't have to give up the things that make you happy. Maybe you can find another way to hold on to them without adding to your space and taking away from your wallet. (Note my math reference to addition and subtraction. See, math does come in handy!) Many times, simplicity is the way to go.

Also, there is a constant evolution of technology. Records and 8 tracks turned into cassette tapes, which turned into CD's. Now, music is in the cloud.

A flat screen tv was once something only the rich could afford. Today, they are thinner and cheaper than ever. VCRs, DVD players, and typewriters are uncommon. We now watch what we want on streaming services while many, including myself, have found that cutting cable wasn't as bad as I thought it would be. It's changed my viewing habits. I often pick a show and stick with it versus flipping through channels to find something I would want to watch. By the way, whoever invented binge watching is a genius in my opinion. Just saying.

The average American moves at least 11 times in their lifetime (Chandler, 2016). How much easier on your back, and yes, your wallet would it be to have less stuff? Give yourself permission to let your life be as simple as you want. Uncomplicate it.

In this segment on quantity, I would be remiss if I didn't talk about retail therapy. No, I'm not going to try to talk you out of shopping. What I will suggest is substituting. If you're feeling like you want to shop for fun, maybe buy something smaller. Look for a less expensive alternative. It can still satisfy your desire for retail therapy without doing too much damage to your wallet.

Another suggestion to address retail therapy issues is to unsubscribe to your store email notifications. If you don't know there's a sale happening, then you won't shop for what you didn't know was out there. Remove the temptation.

And, if you're online shopping and looking to purchase an item that is not a need, try waiting a day or two before placing your order. This may reduce impulse purchases.

Money Movement Plan

Simplify your life.

Pick something in your life to simplify. Whether it's going through old clothes that you don't wear anymore and donating them or cutting a service you don't use often, there are always ways to simplify your life. For example, maybe you subscribe to several streaming services. Do you use all of them each month? Maybe you can try using one streaming service at a time and choose to watch what's available on that particular platform. By the time you're ready to use another streaming service as your primary provider, you may even have more seasons of the shows you're interested in to watch.

Research

Research

Research

Research

Learn all you can before making important decisions. Making informed decisions is always a smart move.

Here's a scenario where someone did their homework:

Bill enjoys camping. He wants to buy new camping equipment for an upcoming trip. He did lots of online research. He looked at what materials tents were made of so he could figure out which might be sturdier and would last longer. He looked at product reviews, prices, and how big the items were so he could get an idea of how much storage space he would need when the equipment wasn't in use. He also asked friends who shared his love of camping what their thoughts were. And these days, since there are so many social media outlets, Bill posed some questions on his town's Facebook page to see if anyone had recommendations.

Bill did some solid research. Not only did he use the internet to find out all he could about the products he was interested in, but he also asked friends and neighbors for their opinions from their own personal experiences.

Research is good. But you should keep something in mind . . . know your sources.

During the political drama of 2020, Americans discovered that they could find sources that would support their political beliefs, no matter what they were, whether it was an extreme right opinion, a far left extreme, or something that lived in between. What I'm trying to say is . . . *use information from trusted sources.*

When you research, are you looking at credible websites? Is the person you're getting your information from someone who is respected and has experience on the subject at hand?

Generally speaking, when someone seeks you out, that may be an indicator they want something from you. Perhaps they are trying to sell you something, or maybe they want information they can use to their benefit. Not everyone has an ulterior motive. However, you should be deliberate and discerning in your researching efforts.

There is something called the CRAAP test that may be a useful tool. It's an acronym that stands for Currency, Relevance, Authority, Accuracy, and Purpose. It provides a list of questions to ask yourself when deciding whether or not a source is reliable and credible (Website research, 2021).

<u>**Money Movement Plan**</u>

Pick a money related subject and research it. Perhaps your refrigerator is older and showing signs of giving out. If this is the case, research refrigerators in preparation for needing a new one.

Once you've completed your research task, ask yourself:

- Was it easy to research?
- How many sources did you check?
- Did you only do your research online, or did you check with another resource, like maybe a friend who went through a similar experience?
- Were they trusted sources?
- What did you learn?

Savings

Life happens. Jobs can be lost. Health issues can pop up. **There will be unexpected expenses.** Save for retirement. Social Security won't be enough. Save for personal goals, like vacations, celebrations, anniversaries. Have an emergency fund.

Most importantly, save yourself!

Having more savings will help you to feel confident and protected. Don't rely on someone else to get you out of a jam. They may not be willing, or able, to help.

If you are in a position where putting aside money is easier said than done, then let's talk about ways to make it happen.

First, get organized. If you've already created your budget, then it will be easier to get yourself organized. Analyze your categories. Where are you spending the most money? Do you see areas where you can make spending cuts? Make necessary cuts and then put that newfound money towards savings.

Second, don't underestimate the power of accumulation. Little things can add up quickly. For a week, try to look for ways to save. Use coupons at the grocery store and/or buy a generic product in place of a brand name. If you buy coffee daily, choose to make it at home instead. Call your internet provider and try to negotiate a better rate. At the end of the week, figure out how much these small changes have added up to. If you continue these changes, how much would you save in a month? A year? Again, put that newfound money towards savings.

Next, pay yourself first. Set *up automatic deposits.*
Put money aside and don't think about it. Commit
to not touching it unless you really need to.

As your income increases, like if you get yearly
raises at work, consider putting at least a portion
towards your savings until it's built up. The same
idea applies if you get a work bonus or a tax refund.

If you're still finding that putting aside savings is
slow going, *consider getting a second source of
income,* even if it's just for a little while until you
have an adequate amount put aside.

Once you've reached your goal, celebrate the win!
You deserve it! But, there's also no harm in
continuing to save even if you have reached your
goal. When was the last time you heard someone
complain that they have too much money?

Money Movement Plan

Don't underestimate the power of accumulation.

For a week, look for ways to save.
- At the end of the week, calculate how much these small changes amounted to.
- If you continue these changes, how much would you save in a month? A year?
- Put any newfound money towards savings.
- How long will it take to reach your savings goal?

Taxes

Taxes are a part of life. Taxes pay police officers, public servants, and teachers among many other things. Taxes help to keep our society running.

Some well-known men had the following to say about taxes:

"The only two certainties in life are death and taxes." *Benjamin Franklin, Founding Father of the U.S.*

"The problem is not that the people are taxed too little. The problem is that government spends too much." *President Ronald Reagan, Republican*

"What people really want is fairness. They want people paying their fair share of taxes." *President Barack Obama, Democrat*

Americans pay several types of taxes. Although we have federal taxes in common, states and local governments also tax by their own standards. For example, many states have a personal income tax (only a handful do not). Even then, tax rates differ among the individual jurisdictions themselves. There can be property tax, sales tax, estate tax, gift tax, and excise tax, among others. Depending on where you live, you may be paying some of the above taxes, all the above taxes, or maybe even a few more not specifically mentioned here.

Given the variety of taxes that are levied, how many people look at the budgets where these monies are being allocated? Have you ever looked at your town or state budget? Do you only think about it when there's a problem, meaning there's not enough money to cover expenses and now the gap in the budget needs to be addressed? With all the disagreements over money, why aren't we looking at what taxes are funding? Sure, we might be told something general like it's going to repair highways. Ok. How much of it is going to repair highways? How long will these repairs take? What happens if there's a shortage and more money is needed for repairs? Then where will the difference come from? And, what if there's an overage? Where does the excess money go to then? How long before the roads need to be repaired again?

Who's asking questions? If you're not, don't feel bad. I don't think many people do, but that doesn't mean we should stay the course. Get involved in your community. Even a simple suggestion like changing from mailing a physical letter to a digital email when a notification policy needs to be sent can save money. Multiply that savings by the total number of recipients.

Just as we should educate ourselves on individual matters, we should educate ourselves on community matters. If you're saying to yourself, I don't have time for that, I understand. But what is the cost of inaction? If you put a dollar figure to it and it's big enough, would you make time for it then? Getting involved could promote accountability as well.

Money Movement Plan

Look at your state or local budget. I'm not asking you to become a financial analyst. Just open it up, look at it, and find out where taxes are being allocated and how much are being allocated to each category. Maybe you can attend a budget meeting. If you have questions or suggestions, perhaps you can reach out to a local representative to discuss.

U

Understanding

For me, there are subjects that seem hard to grasp, like chemistry. Science is not my strong suit. So, it would be reasonable to assume I would not know much about toxicology for instance. However, if there were a toxicology related issue that affected me personally, one of the first things I would do is research the subject.

With financial matters, some subjects are unavoidable. For instance, we are continually paying taxes, having insurance is in a person's best interest, and we know we should be saving for retirement since Social Security won't be enough to cover the bills once we do officially retire. It would be in your best interest to educate yourself on a subject if it personally affects you.

As a case in point, if you don't prepare your own taxes each year, there's absolutely nothing wrong with that and you are definitely not alone. Even Albert Einstein found income taxes difficult to understand.

You can hire a tax accountant, but you should still know enough about the subject to know how your choices affect your personal situation.

As another example, we know that putting money away for retirement is a good idea. Do you know what types of accounts are available to save for retirement and how they differ? Do you know the difference between a Traditional IRA and a Roth IRA? A simple Google search will tell you that a Traditional IRA allows you to make pre-tax contributions. Your money grows tax-deferred, and withdrawals are taxed as current income after age 59½. A Roth IRA allows you to make after tax contributions. Your money grows tax-free, and you can generally make tax and penalty-free withdrawals after age 59½ (Roth IRA Vs, n.d.).

There are many resources at your disposal. An internet search is the first thing that comes to mind, but don't exclude other sources, like performing research at your local library or consulting an expert on a specific subject.

Sometimes you might even feel pressured to buy something. Perhaps someone is trying to convince you to make a particular purchase. Don't feel pressured. It's your money! If you don't understand something, or don't feel comfortable, then educate yourself or don't do it if it's optional! Understand the reasoning behind your choices. Understand the reasoning behind someone else's push. Do they have something to gain? What is their motivation? Do they work off commissions perhaps?

Work to understand how your decision on a particular subject will affect you. It can only help!

<u>**Money Movement Plan**</u>

*Pick a particular money related subject that you
don't know much about.* It could be insurance,
retirement, or anything else.

- Educate yourself on the subject.
- List pros and cons.
- List your options.
- If it's a subject that personally affects you,
  what are the best decisions you can make to
  improve your situation?

V

Variable Expenses

Variable expenses are expenses that change. They are not consistent. Variable expenses are things like entertainment, food, gifts, and commuting expenses among other categories.

	Food	Clothes	Entertainment
January	$450	$75	$200
February	$390	$0	$150
March	$475	$100	$250
April	$525	$150	$375
May	$440	$0	$225

Avoid unnecessary expenses if you can't afford it, especially if you don't have an emergency fund or you're not saving enough for retirement. *Keep your spending in check!*

It can be easy for variable expenses to get away from you. For example, being invited to a wedding can easily add a considerable amount to anyone's budget. A new outfit and a wedding gift can be a sizable expense.

But you can stay on top of at least some of your variable expenses. Maybe you can have a game night at home with friends versus eating out at a restaurant to reduce your entertainment expenses. Or, if the weather is nice, go to the park for a hike versus opting to see a movie at your local movie theater. This is another place where substitution can work wonders. You don't have to deprive yourself of having fun. Sometimes you just have to come up with other ways to achieve what you want.

Groceries are also another place where purchases can add up quickly. Maybe buying generic brands might have to be sufficient until you can build up adequate savings. It's a temporary adjustment that can help you meet your goals.

Money Movement Plan

Look at your budget.

- Where do you spend the most money when it comes to variable expenses?
- Do you see room for improvement? What can you do to get there?

Are there any substitutions you can and are willing to make, even temporarily, so you can put aside some savings?

Wants

A want is something you would like to have but may not be necessary. It's ok to purchase things you want, *as long as you can afford it!*

I think most adults understand the difference between what's a "need" and what's a "want." It's the difference between what's essential and what is not. So, let's try another Money Movement Game!

Money Movement Game

The following word search puzzle contains eight words that are "wants."

See if you can find them.

K P C V G S D C

L I X A J O L O

G U M C E D F N

O E R A W A E C

L R F T O Y S E

F D G I V M U R

Y A N O T Z D T

B Q H N M K I B

J E W E L R Y D

Answer:

```
K   P   C   V   G   S   D   C
L   I   X   A   J   O   L   O
G   U   M   C   E   D   F   N
O   E   R   A   W   A   E   C
L   R   F   T   O   Y   S   E
F   D   G   I   V   M   U   R
Y   A   N   O   T   Z   D   T
B   Q   H   N   M   K   I   B
J   E   W   E   L   R   Y   D
```

X

Xmas and Other Gift Giving Occasions

It really is the thought that counts! So, don't go broke buying gifts. No one wants that.

When it comes to gifts, what makes them special usually has to do with who is giving the gift and the thoughtfulness behind it. A memorable gift often comes from someone who has good intentions. It's not about the dollar value attached to the gift.

A great gift makes you feel good. It also might make you feel closer to the person giving it, as it may make you feel like they understand you and want to make you happy. You can look at a gift and be reminded of that person and of their kindness.

The idea behind gift giving is not the more you spend, the better the gift. You don't have to go into debt to show your love or appreciation for someone in your life.

A thoughtful act or gesture can be considered a gift. Homemade cookies, a handmade scarf, or someone preparing dinner for you are all kind and considerate gestures. You may not be able to wrap some of the things that aren't considered traditional gifts, but they are appreciated, nonetheless.

I'm not suggesting that you stop buying gifts in the traditional sense. Just stay within the boundaries of what you're able to afford.

> **"The richest gifts we can bestow are the least marketable."**
> **Henry David Thoreau**

Money Movement Plan

Set a monetary limit on the next gift you plan to buy.

- If what you purchase doesn't seem like enough, come up with something creative to balance out the gift.
- You can make something or perhaps offer something like babysitting or pet sitting services the next time that person is looking for a sitter.

Y

Youth

Time is an important advantage in terms of finances. The sooner you start saving, investing, and thinking about your financial future, the better.

When you consider compound interest, which is when you receive interest on top of interest, your savings grows quicker (Introduction to, n.d.). So, a savings account with compound interest is preferable to an account with simple interest, which is only based on the principal amount (Nickolas, 2020).

Here's an example of how compound interest works:

- If you have $100 in savings at a 4% interest rate, you will receive $4 in interest. When this interest is added to your base savings, you have $104.

- Now, the $104 becomes your base savings. When you apply 4% interest to the $104, your interest becomes $4.16. $104 plus $4.16 equals $108.16, which is your new base.

And this repeats.

If this scenario continues, after 10 years, your savings will amount to $148.02. After 20 years, your savings will amount to $219.11. And so, the advantage of saving early becomes a little easier to see.

In a very different scenario, let's say you have an investment that is doing poorly-- meaning you're losing money. If you have more time, you can wait for your investment to potentially improve or perhaps work to make up for the losses incurred.

Another thing to consider is if you start forming good financial habits early, you're creating positive behavior. The continuance of this "good behavior" can give you the structure you need to be successful in terms of managing your money.

Speaking of positives, some employers will match a certain percentage of money you put towards a 401k at your place of work. This is money that will otherwise be lost if you don't take advantage of it. So, it would be wise to put away at least the percentage amount where you would qualify for the full employer match. Also, saving earlier can give you more time to save for your goals. Let's say you're now 22 years old and you want to buy a house by age 32. You know you have 10 years to save. If you put away $100 a week, you'll have $5,200 a year. Multiply that by 10 years and that's $52,000. Not too shabby! But, if you start saving at 29 years of age and still want to buy a house by age 32, you'll have saved $15,600--significantly less.

You may even have to consider postponing some goals if you just don't have enough money or time to save.

All in all, starting your financial journey early is the way to go. But, if you haven't started early, you may still be able to reach your goals with a little more effort. Or, you may have to make some compromises and reevaluate your plans.

As you get older and accumulate wealth and assets, don't forget to do things like get life insurance if you have people who are financially dependent on you and create a Will. One in three families didn't have life insurance coverage in 2020 (Life insurance statistics, 2021). If you do have coverage, is it enough or are you underinsured?

Even if you don't have a lot of assets, a Will is still a
good idea. Your wishes will be made clear. If you
have minor children, it's especially important. Also,
ensure that someone knows where to find the
original document.

Money Movement Plan

Look for quotes about money and wealth.

- Pick one that speaks to you.
- Write it on a piece of paper and put it on your fridge or somewhere you'll see it regularly.
- Let it be a reminder of why you started this financial quest.

Z

Zillionaire

If you want to be a zillionaire, you've got to start somewhere!

Adulting can be hard at any age. It would be so much easier if you didn't have to worry about finances. Sure, thinking about moving to a remote island and living off the land may sound fun for a minute, but then I would miss things like snow in the winter and pizza in the northeast. And how would I binge watch shows on Netflix if I didn't have electricity to plug in my television, modem, and router?

Money is a necessity for many things in life. Learning to manage your finances in a way that provides you comfort and security is an accomplishment. Providing for yourself, and possibly for others, is a way of showing love. It is a gift!

Build financial security and gain peace of mind.

Gather your information, plan, organize, prioritize, and choose wisely. Being human, you're bound to make some mistakes. It's ok. Reassess, readjust, and get back on track. You got this!

Money Movement Plan

Start somewhere!

- Preferably, start with a budget.
- Then move forward . . . one step at a time.

Not every decision

in life is based on

finances ...

but you should be aware

of the financial

implications of every

decision.

Now you know your ABCs

Work to become financially free.

Get it together, and you can feel as light as a feather.

Medicine
Student Loans
Kids
Utilities
Unexpected Expenses
Food
Vacations
Rent
EMERGENCY
Pets
Need New Glasses
Retirement
Investments
Car Payments
Last Will and Testament
Clothing
Tax
Life Insurance
Dentist Visit
Eating Out
Car Maintenance
Health Insurance
Doctor's Appointment
Charitable donations
Mortgage
Entertainment
Emergency Fund
Subscriptions
Credit Card Debt

Bonus

Numbers

1 2 3

The one person who will have the most impact on your financial situation is you!

1

Your choices and decisions will have consequences. Your efforts shape your financial reality.

Remember that being honest with yourself about your financial situation is essential.

Two questions to ask yourself when you are about to spend money:

Need 2 Want

Do you need it? Or Do you want it?

Figuring out what emotionally drives your decisions plays a significant part in your financial picture. Consider this aspect.

Three strategies to make a budget work:

3

1. Cut your expenses
2. Increase your income
3. A combination of cutting expenses and increasing income

Wishing you a bright and financially independent future!

References

Account Summary. (n.d.). https://client.schwab.com/Login/SignOn/CustomerCenterLogin.aspx?ReturnUrl=%2fclientapps%2faccounts%2fsummary%2f&SessionTimeOut=Y

Barrett, J. (2018). Why We Fight Over Money so Much, and How to Stop. https://www.forbes.com/sites/jenniferbarrett/2018/01/17/why-we-fight-over-money-so-much-and-how-to-stop/?sh=1d21a72812b4

Capital Budget. (n.d.) 2000-2019.https://portal.ct.gov/-/media/OPM/Budget/2018_2019_Biennial_Budget/BudgetDocs/041SectionDpdf.pdf

Chakrovorty, D . (2016). Most Popular People Born in 1950s. https://www.imdb.com/list/ls066014918

Chandler, A. (2016). Why do americans move so much more than europeans? https://www.theatlantic.com/business/archive/2016/10/us-geographic-mobility/504968/#:~:text=According%20to%20data%20from%20the,in%20his%20or%20her%20lifetime

DeNicola, L. (2020). 9 Ways Your Credit Score Affects Your Everyday Life. https://studentloanhero.com/featured/surpris

ing-ways-your-credit-score-affects-your-everyday-life/

Dennison, S. (2019). 64% of Americans Aren't Prepared For Retirement — and 48% Don't Care. https://finance.yahoo.com/news/survey-finds-42-americans-retire-100701878.html?guccounter=1&guce_referrer=aHR0cHM6Ly93d3cuZ29vZ2xlLmNvbS8&guce_referrer_sig=AQAAAJlT9hCePRvRm1mBJF2mHAStXZ5rPMqgBi5VhlsEsCy4va5sW-7atjjwxLw1d5owCgI0eDC3vBshkFlKN30QA5tn5VRA7FEWNw8-UFifl_nMHisOK5wuR5V7Z4lnEY2Wenzmq8FYQMxV8VgD6EFCouAcsqDZjmYJGFgXNue6n9n0

Dividend. (2021). https://www.bankrate.com/glossary/d/dividend/

Fernando, J. (2021). Dividend Yield. https://www.investopedia.com/terms/d/dividendyield.asp#:~:text=The%20dividend%20yield%E2%80%93displayed%20as,by%20its%20current%20stock%20price

Here's a List of 20 Inventions in the 1950s. (n.d.). https://nevadainventors.org/20-inventions-1950s/

Horch, A. (2020). Almost Half of America is Now Carrying Credit Card Debt, and More of It. https://www.cnbc.com/2020/05/04/almost-half-of-america-now-carrying-credit-card-

debt-and-more-of-
it.html#:~:text=Nearly%20half%20(47%25)%2
0of,new%20report%20from%20CreditCards.c
om

Howard, B. (2009). 17 Things You Didn't Know
You Could Rent.
https://www.goodhousekeeping.com/life/mon
ey/advice/g2210/renting-things-461009/

Huddleston, C. (2019). Survey: 69% of
Americans Have Less Than $1,000 in Savings.
https://www.gobankingrates.com/saving-
money/savings-advice/americans-have-less-
than-1000-in-savings/

Introduction to investing. (n.d.).
https://www.investor.gov/additional-
resources/information/youth/teachers-
classroom-resources/what-compound-
interest#:~:text=Compound%20interest%20is
%20the%20interest,%2C%20you%27ll%20hav
e%20%24110.25

Life insurance statistics and data: Industry
facts, figures, and data. (2021).
https://www.bestliferates.org/life-insurance-
statistics/

Morad, R. (2021). 46 Million Americans Wiped
Out Their Emergency Savings During the
Pandemic--How to Turn it All Around in 2021.
https://www.nbcnews.com/know-your-
value/feature/46-million-americans-wiped-
out-their-emergency-savings-during-
pandemic-ncna1254073

Nickolas, S. (2020). Simple interest vs compound interesthttps://www.investopedia.com/ask/answers/042315/what-difference-between-compounding-interest-and-simple-interest.asp#:~:text=The%20interest%2C%20typically%20expressed%20as,on%20it%20in%20every%20period.

9 Positive Effects of Donating Money to Charity. (2015). https://www.thelifeyoucansave.org/blog/9-positive-effects-of-donating-money-to-charity/

Paolini, C. (2011) Inheritance. Alfred K. Knopf.

Passengers left more than $900k behind at TSA security checkpoints. (2020). https://www.tsa.gov/news/press/releases/2020/08/21/passengers-left-more-900k-behind-tsa-security-checkpoints

Roth IRA vs Traditional IRA. (n.d.). https://www.schwab.com/ira/understand-iras/roth-vs-trad-ira#:~:text=With%20a%20Roth%20IRA%2C%20you,current%20income%20after%20age%2059%C2%BD

Royal, J. (2020). What is the Average Stock Market Return? https://www.nerdwallet.com/article/investing/average-stock-market-return

SMART goal. (2015).
https://corporatefinanceinstitute.com/resourc
es/knowledge/other/smart-
goal/#:~:text=A%20SMART%20goal%20is%2
0used,chances%20of%20achieving%20your%2
0goal

The Complete History of Credit Cards, From
Antiquity to Today. (2020).
https://thepointsguy.com/guide/history-of-
credit-cards/

Travelers leave behind $960,105 in unclaimed
money at TSA checkpoints in FY2018. (n.d.).
60105-unclaimed-money-tsa-checkpoints-
fy2018

Website research. Central Michigan University.
(2021).
https://libguides.cmich.edu/web_research/cra
ap#:~:text=The%20test%20provides%20a%20
list,more%20information%2C%20please%20se
e%20below

Additional Resources

Bankrate.com

Consumer Financial Protection Bureau (consumerfinance.gov)

Consumer Reports Guide to Health Insurance (consumerreports.org/health-insurance/guide-to-health-insurance/

FINRA BrokerCheck (brokercheck.finra.org)

Investopedia.com

Mint.com

Morningstar Investing Classroom (morningstar.com/start-investing/classroom)

StudentLoans.gov